E SCIENCE

FREAKY STORIES ABOUT OUR BODIES

BY KRISTEN RAJCZAK

 Gareth Stevens
PUBLISHING

Please visit our website, www.garethstevens.com. For a free color catalog of all our high-quality books, call toll free 1-800-542-2595 or fax 1-877-542-2596.

Library of Congress Cataloging-in-Publication Data

Rajczak, Kristen, author.
Freaky stories about our bodies / Kristen Rajczak.
    pages cm — (Freaky true science)
Includes bibliographical references and index.
ISBN 978-1-4824-2960-2 (pbk.)
ISBN 978-1-4824-2961-9 (6 pack)
ISBN 978-1-4824-2962-6 (library binding)
1. Medicine—Miscellanea—Juvenile literature. 2. Human body—Miscellanea—Juvenile literature. 3. Medical innovations—Juvenile literature. I. Title.
R706.R35 2016
610.2—dc23

                                                2015007002

First Edition

Published in 2016 by
Gareth Stevens Publishing
111 East 14th Street, Suite 349
New York, NY 10003

Copyright © 2016 Gareth Stevens Publishing

Designer: Sarah Liddell
Editor: Ryan Nagelhout

Photo credits: Cover, p. 1 (leg and arm used throughout book) Morphart Creation/ Shutterstock.com; cover, pp. 1 (fingernails), 7 (Chris Walton) STAN HONDA/Staff/AFP/ Getty Images; cover, background throughout book Graphic design/Shutterstock.com; pp. 5, 7, 9, 11, 13, 15, 17, 19, 21, 23, 25, 27, 29 (hand used throughout) Helena Ohman/ Shutterstock.com; pp. 5, 7, 9, 11, 13, 15, 17, 19, 21, 23, 25, 27, 29 (texture throughout) Alex Gontar/Shutterstock.com; p. 5 Boston Globe/Contributor/Boston Globe/Getty Images; p. 7 (normal cells) Onur Gunduz/Shutterstock.com; p. 7 (cancer cells) Lightspring/ Shutterstock.com; p. 7 (Chris Walton) STAN HONDA/Staff/AFP/Getty Images; p. 8 MedicalRF.com/Getty Images; p. 9 Scimat Scimat/Science Source/Getty Images; p. 11 Biophoto Associates -/Science Source/Getty Images; p. 12 Scewing/Wikimedia Commons; pp. 13, 24 Barcroft/Contributor/Barcroft Media/Getty Images; p. 15 (brain scan) Medical Body Scans/Science Source/Getty Images; p. 15 (nerves) Rallwel/ Shutterstock.com; p. 17 microgen/E+/Getty Images; p. 18 Arsgera/Shutterstock.com; p. 19 Harry Kikstra/Moment/Getty Images; p. 21 Bill Ingalls/NASA/Handout/ Getty Images News/Getty Images; p. 23 Materialscientist/Wikimedia Commons; p. 25 Getty Images/Handout/Getty Images News/Getty Images; p. 27 (Blade Runner) RubberBall Productions/Brand X Pictures/Getty Images; p. 27 (eye) Entheta/ Wikimedia Commons; p. 29 J. R. Eyerman/Contributor/The LIFE Picture Collection/ Getty Images.

Printed in the United States of America

CPSIA compliance information: Batch #CS15GS. For further information contact Gareth Stevens, New York, New York at 1-800-542-2595.

CONTENTS

Words in the glossary appear in **bold** type
the first time they are used in the text.

A NEW FACE

In 2008, a Texas man named Dallas Wiens was painting a building when an electrical wire hit his head. Wiens was burned terribly. He survived, but the skin **grafts** he received on his face healed to just bare flesh where his eyes and nose used to be. For years, Wiens lived with only a mouth opening. That is, until he got a face **transplant**.

The first successful organ transplant, a kidney, was performed in 1954. Since then, millions of people have received lungs, hearts, and many other organs. But it wasn't until 2005 that the first face transplant was attempted. Wiens's was the first full face transplant done in the United States.

There are lots of stories about the human body that are nearly unbelievable! Some are just freaky!

FREAKY FACTS!

About 10 months after his surgery, Wiens was able to smile, smell, and drink from a glass.

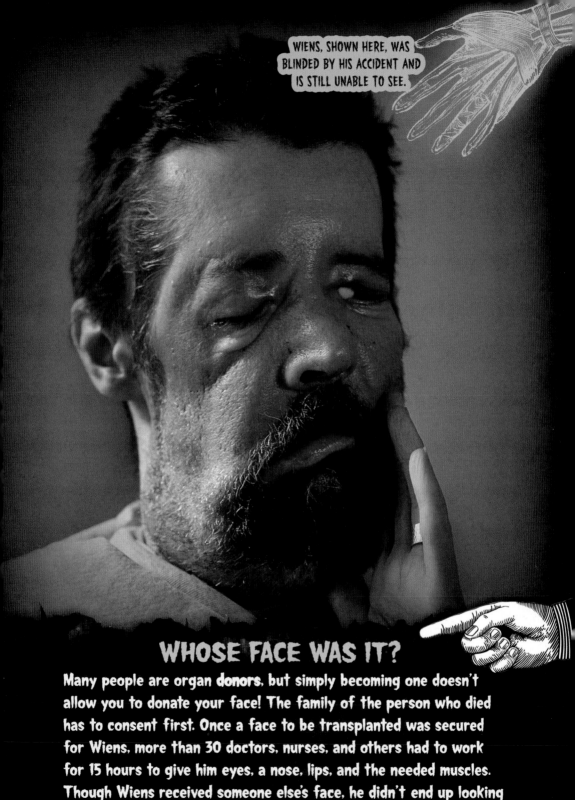

WIENS, SHOWN HERE, WAS BLINDED BY HIS ACCIDENT AND IS STILL UNABLE TO SEE.

WHOSE FACE WAS IT?

Many people are organ **donors**, but simply becoming one doesn't allow you to donate your face! The family of the person who died has to consent first. Once a face to be transplanted was secured for Wiens, more than 30 doctors, nurses, and others had to work for 15 hours to give him eyes, a nose, lips, and the needed muscles. Though Wiens received someone else's face, he didn't end up looking like that person. That would've been freaky!

YOUR UNUSUAL BODY

Many strange stories about the human body tell us about fascinating medical discoveries or disease. There are plenty of those in this book. But let's first look at some everyday functions and truths about your body. Some of it's pretty freaky!

The human body is made up of cells, which are the basic units of life. Yet millions of them die every day! Don't worry: they're supposed to do this. In fact, cells have a plan for their death inside them, just waiting for the signal.

While millions die each day, millions more are being created to replace them. Over the course of about 27 days, you'll **regenerate** the top layer of your skin. The lining of your stomach is replaced in about 3 days!

FREAKY FACTS!

Simply put, cancer is the unchecked growth of abnormal cells. These cells might form a mass, or tumor, and spread to other body parts.

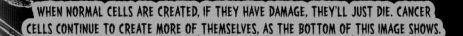

HOW CANCER FORMS

NORMAL CELL

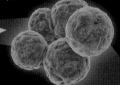

NORMAL CELL GROWTH

TUMORS BUD AND SPREAD THROUGHOUT THE BODY

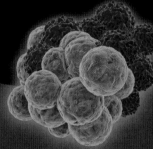

MUTATION RESULTS IN CANCER CELL

CANCER CELL GROWTH FORMS TUMOR

EMBRACING THE WEIRD

Some freaky things about the human body happen naturally. For example, babies are born with almost 100 more bones than adults! Many of them are made of a soft tissue called cartilage and grow together into the 206-bone adult skeleton. Babies' kneecaps are just soft cartilage at first! Some people embrace the natural growth of the body a little too much. Chris Walton broke the world record for longest fingernails in 2012. The nails of her left hand grew to a total of 10 feet 2 inches (3.1 m)!

7

We're outnumbered in our own bodies! Even though your body has trillions of cells, there are about 10 times as many bacterial cells found in and on your body.

Did you know not all bacteria are harmful? While some kinds cause illness, other bacteria help your body work properly. Microorganisms, or microbes, live in your stomach and intestines to help your body break down food into **nutrients** it can use. Others make things the body needs and can't make itself, such as vitamins.

Some people's guts don't have the bacteria they need anymore. Doctors found a pretty freaky way to fix that: **fecal** microbiota transplants (FMTs). To many people—even those who might benefit from an FMT—this sounds too weird or gross to try.

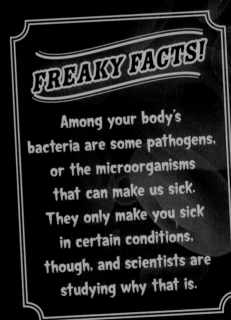

FREAKY FACTS!

Among your body's bacteria are some pathogens, or the microorganisms that can make us sick. They only make you sick in certain conditions, though, and scientists are studying why that is.

COMMON STOMACH PATHOGEN, HELICOBACTER PYLORI

FMT

Not many doctors perform FMTs, though the number seems to be growing. In the United States, rules about studying human fecal matter for medical reasons are slowly changing as success from FMTs continues. FMTs have been especially successful for the treatment of an overpopulation of a harmful bacterium called *Clostridium difficile*, or *C. diff*. In an FMT, fecal matter from a donor is tested for the right good bacteria. It's then mixed with salt water, the solids are removed, and it's put into a patient.

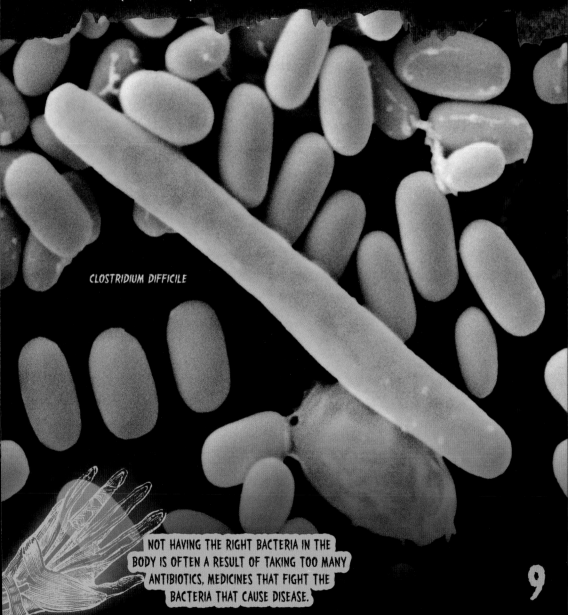

CLOSTRIDIUM DIFFICILE

NOT HAVING THE RIGHT BACTERIA IN THE BODY IS OFTEN A RESULT OF TAKING TOO MANY ANTIBIOTICS, MEDICINES THAT FIGHT THE BACTERIA THAT CAUSE DISEASE.

A STRANGE GENE

Can you tell the difference between red and green? About 1 in 10 men can't! They're color-blind. Color blindness is one fairly common occurrence that's caused by a genetic mutation. No one knows you're color-blind unless you tell them, but some genetic mutations are easy to see.

Antonio Alfonseca was a relief pitcher in Major League Baseball from 1997 to 2007. He has a genetic mutation called polydactyly that caused him to develop a sixth finger before he was born! The finger is small and gave him no advantage when he pitched. Polydactyl people have six or more fingers or toes. It can be inherited, be part of a disease, or simply occur as a mutation on its own. Rarely, people are born with just one finger or toe. That's called monodactyly.

FREAKY FACTS!

Gene mutations can occur suddenly during a person's life, such as a cell making an incomplete copy of itself or if a person is exposed to harmful chemicals.

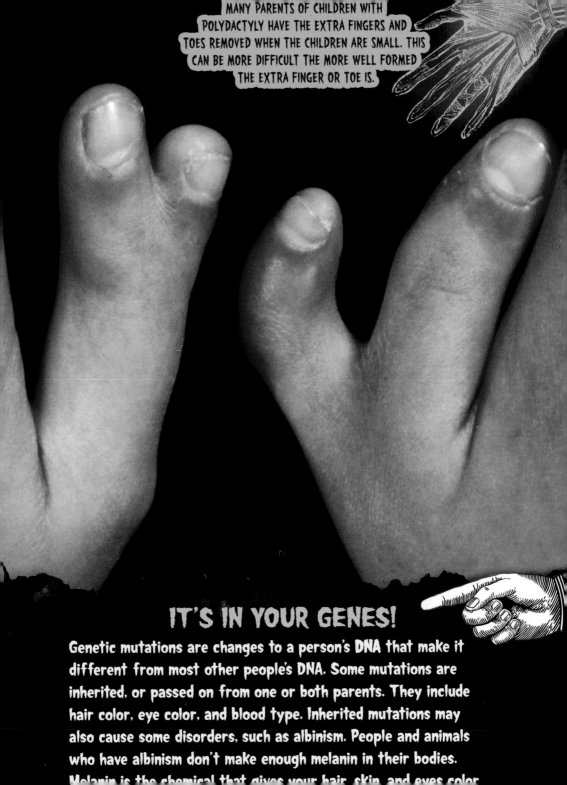

MANY PARENTS OF CHILDREN WITH POLYDACTYLY HAVE THE EXTRA FINGERS AND TOES REMOVED WHEN THE CHILDREN ARE SMALL. THIS CAN BE MORE DIFFICULT THE MORE WELL FORMED THE EXTRA FINGER OR TOE IS.

IT'S IN YOUR GENES!

Genetic mutations are changes to a person's **DNA** that make it different from most other people's DNA. Some mutations are inherited, or passed on from one or both parents. They include hair color, eye color, and blood type. Inherited mutations may also cause some disorders, such as albinism. People and animals who have albinism don't make enough melanin in their bodies. Melanin is the chemical that gives your hair, skin, and eyes color

In 2011, another odd condition with a genetic connection made the news. The Guinness World Record committee named a girl from Thailand as the world's hairiest child. The girl, Supatra Sasuphan, was born with hypertrichosis, which causes excessive growth of hair on the body and face. Only about 50 cases of hypertrichosis, also called Ambras syndrome, have ever been recorded.

Scientists have found that some hypertrichosis runs in families, meaning it's a genetic mutation that can be passed on. Extra genes are found on a specific part of an affected person's DNA. These genes tell the body to keep growing hair.

Scientists might be able to create a drug that will act like the extra genes and turn on the hair growth gene. This discovery could help people with another genetic condition—baldness!

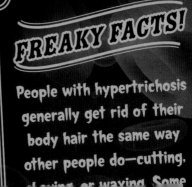

FREAKY FACTS!

People with hypertrichosis generally get rid of their body hair the same way other people do—cutting,

SUPATRA HAS SAID SHE WAS TEASED AND BULLIED BY OTHER KIDS.

REAL WEREWOLVES?

The way hair grows on people with hypertrichosis may have helped start scary stories about werewolves being real! Today, hypertrichosis is even sometimes called "werewolf syndrome." However, we know now that hypertrichosis is inherited or can be caused by chemical imbalances in the body, not by a bite from a wolf during a full moon. Those with the syndrome can't help how their hair grows!

13

UNDER ATTACK

One of the major systems in the body is the immune system. Its job is to defend the body from germs, viruses, and other foreign matter. But what happens if the body thinks its own cells are the invaders?

Autoimmune diseases are those in which the body attacks healthy cells. That's downright scary! Sjögren's (SHOH-gruhnz) syndrome, for example, causes the body to attack and destroy the body parts that produce spit and tears, among other problems.

One of the worst autoimmune diseases is multiple sclerosis (MS). The immune system attacks the body's **nerve** coverings, making the brain unable to properly communicate with the body. In the worst cases, MS patients eventually can't walk without aid. People can live a long time with MS, but there's no cure.

FREAKY FACTS!

Doctors have yet to find out what causes autoimmune diseases. It's likely a combination of genetics, a virus or other infection, and other factors in the world around us.

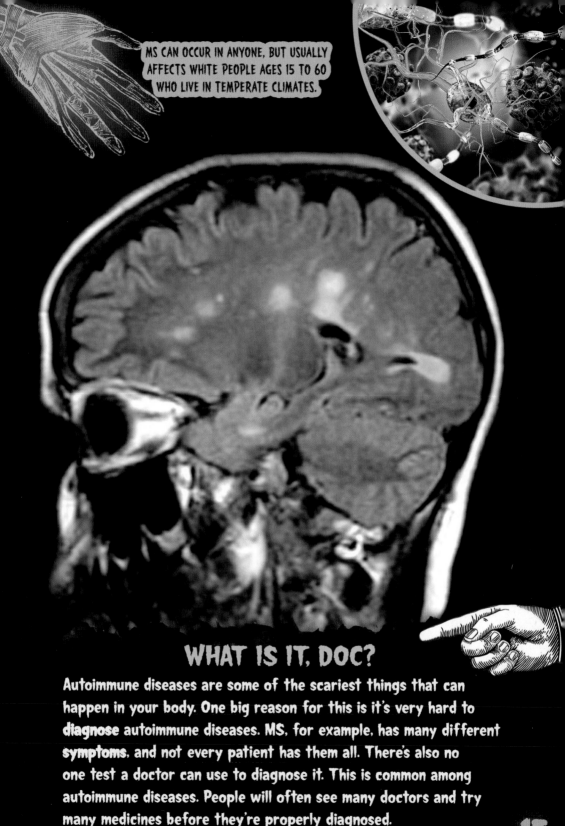

MS CAN OCCUR IN ANYONE, BUT USUALLY AFFECTS WHITE PEOPLE AGES 15 TO 60 WHO LIVE IN TEMPERATE CLIMATES.

WHAT IS IT, DOC?

Autoimmune diseases are some of the scariest things that can happen in your body. One big reason for this is it's very hard to **diagnose** autoimmune diseases. MS, for example, has many different **symptoms**, and not every patient has them all. There's also no one test a doctor can use to diagnose it. This is common among autoimmune diseases. People will often see many doctors and try many medicines before they're properly diagnosed.

15

TO THE EXTREMES

Your body can withstand diving into a few feet of water—and even belly flops. But SCUBA divers may dive down 100 feet (30.5 m) or more! The body starts to get freaky at that depth.

SCUBA divers breathe compressed air from a tank, which contains a small amount of nitrogen the body doesn't use. The deeper divers go, the more pressure there is on the diver and the air in the tank. As this pressure increases, more nitrogen **dissolves** in the body.

As the diver rises, the pressure becomes less, and the body begins to decompress. Surfacing must be done carefully because the dissolved nitrogen is released as bubbles. If the diver comes to the surface too rapidly, the bubbles build up, giving the diver decompression sickness, or the bends.

FREAKY FACTS!

A bottle of soda has bubbles in it, which is pressurized carbon dioxide. When the bottle is opened, bubbles rise to the top. That's what happens when a diver has nitrogen in their tissues and tries to surface too quickly!

FEELING THE DIVE

Divers who are diagnosed with the bends are very uncomfortable after their dive. They'll start having pain around their joints, especially their shoulders and elbows. Extreme tiredness and some difficulty breathing may occur. Sometimes divers go into shock. To prevent getting the bends, divers going very deep should slowly rise to the surface, stopping as they go to let the gas come out of their tissues a little at a time.

THE RISK OF THE BENDS INCREASES THE DEEPER A DIVER GOES.

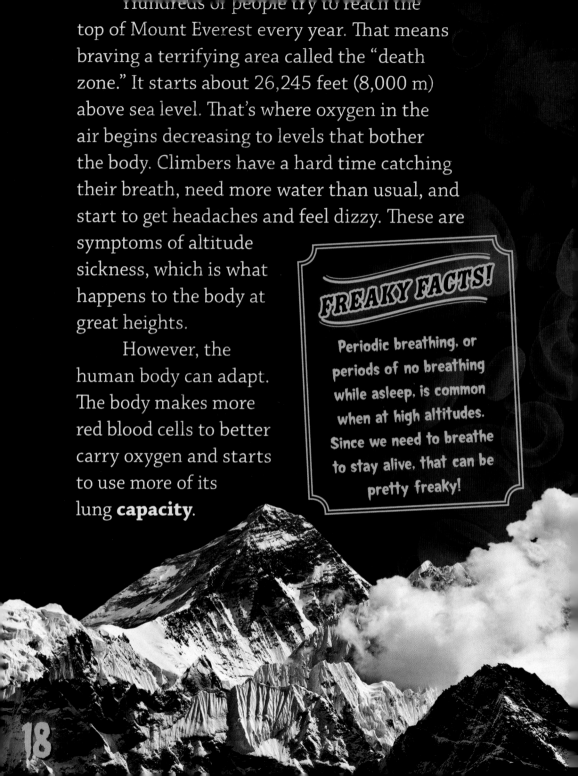

Hundreds of people try to reach the top of Mount Everest every year. That means braving a terrifying area called the "death zone." It starts about 26,245 feet (8,000 m) above sea level. That's where oxygen in the air begins decreasing to levels that bother the body. Climbers have a hard time catching their breath, need more water than usual, and start to get headaches and feel dizzy. These are symptoms of altitude sickness, which is what happens to the body at great heights.

However, the human body can adapt. The body makes more red blood cells to better carry oxygen and starts to use more of its lung **capacity**.

FREAKY FACTS!

Periodic breathing, or periods of no breathing while asleep, is common when at high altitudes. Since we need to breathe to stay alive, that can be pretty freaky!

ONCE CLIMBERS REACH THE "DEATH ZONE,"
THEY'RE RISKING THEIR OWN HEALTH
FOR MOUNTAIN CLIMBING GLORY.

ALTITUDE DEATH

Before attempting the tallest mountains, climbers should climb
smaller ones. This teaches their body how to adapt more quickly
to higher altitudes. In addition, climbers should take weeks to climb
huge mountains like Everest, stopping for days or weeks at the
camps on the mountainsides in order to let their body adapt. Failing
to do either of these things puts climbers at an even greater risk in
the "death zone." Many have, in fact, died because of the altitude.

19

THE HIGHEST HEIGHTS

In March 2015, US astronaut Scott Kelly began a yearlong stretch aboard the International Space Station (ISS). Astronauts have been living aboard the ISS for more than a decade, and scientists have continually monitored how the human body responds to the journey, living in space, and coming home. There are still a lot of unanswered questions, and Scott and his twin brother Mark are hoping to help provide answers.

Mark Kelly, a retired astronaut, will undergo health tests while living his normal life on Earth. Mark's results will then be compared to his genetic copy Scott while he's living in space. They'll continue to be monitored when Scott returns to Earth after the year. The experiment is being called a once-in-a-space-program opportunity for scientists.

FREAKY FACTS!

Scientists are studying the effects of space on the human body with the hope that they could send an astronaut to Mars one day. They guess that would be about an 8-month trip both ways, and they don't know what freaky stuff might happen!

SINCE MARK HAS ALSO BEEN TO SPACE, THE EXPERIMENT ISN'T PERFECT—BUT SINCE SCOTT WILL HAVE BEEN IN SPACE ABOUT 10 TIMES LONGER THAN HIS TWIN, IT'S ABOUT AS CLOSE AS SCIENTISTS CAN EVER HOPE FOR.

S. KELLY
C. КЕЛЛИ

SICK IN SPACE

Astronauts are able to adjust to zero gravity. However, about 40 percent throw up right when they reach space. That usually stops, but dizziness and a tired feeling may remain. In addition, astronauts have increased blood pressure, muscle loss, and likely many other problems that scientists don't know about yet! Everything about those living aboard the ISS is recorded for further study into how space affects the human body, including their bathroom habits!

BORN TOGETHER

On December 12, 2014, twins Carter and Conner Mirabel were born in Florida. These aren't just any twins, though. Carter and Conner are conjoined twins, born joined from the chest to the stomach. Conjoined twins are rare, occurring in only one out of every 200,000 births.

Carter and Conner had their first surgery just 3 days after their birth. In early January 2015, their small intestines were separated. Doctors found out during these surgeries that the boys had separate livers, but the organs had grown together. The doctors will wait until the boys are a little older to attempt separating them fully.

Separating conjoined twins is a difficult undertaking, but Carter and Conner are a type of conjoined twins called omphalopagus. This type of conjoined twins has had some of the most successful separation surgeries.

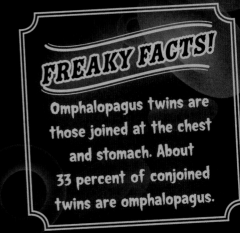

FREAKY FACTS!

Omphalopagus twins are those joined at the chest and stomach. About 33 percent of conjoined twins are omphalopagus.

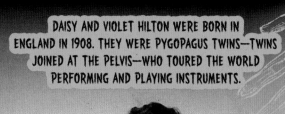

DAISY AND VIOLET HILTON WERE BORN IN
ENGLAND IN 1908. THEY WERE PYGOPAGUS TWINS—TWINS
JOINED AT THE PELVIS—WHO TOURED THE WORLD
PERFORMING AND PLAYING INSTRUMENTS.

HOW DOES IT HAPPEN?

Twins are two babies born at the same time. Identical twins come from one egg that splits and two babies develop with the exact same DNA. Conjoined twins also come from one fertilized egg, but the dividing egg fails to fully separate. About 35 percent of conjoined twins don't live longer than a day. The total survival rate of conjoined twins is about 5 to 25 percent. Whether they can be surgically separated depends on what organs and body functions they share.

Krista and Tatiana Hogan were born in 2006, joined at the side of the head and part of their forehead. Amazingly, they were born healthy and stable, aside from their conjoined heads. Trying to separate two otherwise healthy little girls was a big risk, and their parents decided against it.

If conjoined twins are rare, those joined at the head, called craniopagus twins, are nearly impossible. Only about 2 percent of conjoined twins are craniopagus! But the Hogan girls are remarkable even among craniopagus twins: their brains are connected! Images of their brains show a piece of tissue one doctor believes connects one girl's thalamus to the other girl's thalamus. This means what Krista sees, Tatiana can name when she's blindfolded. When Tatiana drinks, Krista can feel it.

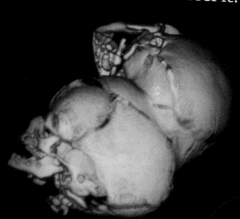

JOINED SKULLS OF
CRANIOPAGUS TWINS

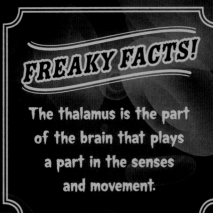

FREAKY FACTS!

The thalamus is the part
of the brain that plays
a part in the senses
and movement.

EACH PAIR OF CONJOINED TWINS HAS UNIQUE CHALLENGES. SOME WILL DIE IF NOT SEPARATED, WHILE OTHERS MAY DIE DURING SURGERY.

SEPARATE, BUT UNEQUAL

Some craniopagus twins must be separated. In the case of two New York boys, Clarence and Carl Aguirre, doctors worried both twins would die if they didn't act. Clarence and Carl shared a part of their brain that had to be carefully divided. They were 2 years old when the tops of their heads were separated, and it was mostly successful. Today, Clarence has few health problems, but Carl has many health issues and likely permanent problems walking and talking.

PHANTOM LIMBS

Some people have parts of their body amputated, or removed, after a bad car accident or because of disease. Amputation is often a good thing. It may be done to stop an infection from spreading or to help a person recover from an accident more quickly. They might be able to do more activities over time than if they still had a crushed arm or leg that just wouldn't heal correctly.

But there's a truly freaky side to amputation—phantom limb syndrome. Amputees report feeling tingling, pain, heat or cold, and other odd sensations where their amputated body part once was. It's not certain why this happens, but some doctors think the brain is using the body's nerves to try to reconnect with the lost limb.

FREAKY FACTS!

The first reports of phantom limb syndrome came from a French surgeon in 1552. He wrote that soldiers with amputated limbs complained of pain in their missing arms and legs.

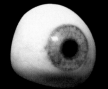

SCIENTISTS ARE WORKING ON MANY DIFFERENT KINDS OF PROSTHETICS. THERE ARE EVEN PROSTHETIC EYES!

PROSTHETIC EYE

PROSTHETICS

Many people around the world use prosthetics—or man-made replacement limbs—to walk and move more normally. A group called Amputee Blade Runners gives free running prosthetics to athletes who have lost a leg or were born without one. One of the group's founders, Ryan Fann, wanted to help change the lives of runners around the United States in the same way his was. Fann was given a prosthetic leg for running after high school and went on to run track at Tennessee State University!

DEEP FREEZE

As time goes on, some of the freaky things scientists have learned about our bodies won't seem so freaky anymore! However, even stranger stories may replace the ones in this book.

The growing field of cryogenics could bring about some of these oddities. Cryogenics is the study of what happens at very low temperatures. Freezing human blood and body tissue may become a common practice. Cryosurgery, or freezing parts of the body to destroy diseased body tissue, is already used to treat cancer and skin problems.

Some freaky stories about our bodies come from our ability to heal, and some of them arise from the amazing medical knowledge we have. What's clear in all these freaky stories is that the human body can withstand a great deal and still survive.

FREAKY FACTS!

A zoo in Louisiana has frozen parts from endangered species, or animals with low world populations! They hope to bring them back if they go extinct.

CRYONICS HAS BEEN AROUND SINCE THE 1960s. IT'S SOMEWHAT LIKE MODERN-DAY MUMMIFICATION!

CRYONICS

In Clinton Township, Michigan, a building houses more than 100 dead bodies. These bodies float in huge tanks of nitrogen kept around −202°F (−130°C). Cryonics is the practice of freezing the human body after death, often with the goal of bringing it back to life once science knows how to cure certain diseases. Baseball player Ted Williams famously had his head frozen after he died. His family hopes he can one day be brought back to life.

GLOSSARY

capacity: the ability to hold or contain

diagnose: to identify a disease

dissolve: to mix completely into a liquid

DNA: molecules in the body that carry genetic information, which gives the instructions for life

donor: someone used as the source of body tissue

fecal: having to do with feces, or solid human waste

graft: a piece of human tissue attached to the body

nerve: a part of the body that carries messages between the brain and other parts of the body

nutrient: something a living thing needs to grow and stay alive

regenerate: to replace by a new growth of tissue

symptom: a sign that shows someone is sick

tissue: matter that forms the parts of living things

transplant: a medical procedure in which an organ is taken from one person and placed in or on another

FOR MORE INFORMATION

BOOKS

De la Bédoyère, Camilla. *Ripley's Believe It or Not: Human Body.* Broomall, PA: Mason Crest, 2011.

Perish, Patrick. *Disgusting Bodily Functions.* Minneapolis, MN: Bellwether Media, Inc., 2014.

Wilsdon, Christina, Patricia Daniels, and Jen Agresta. *Ultimate Body-pedia: An Amazing Inside-Out Tour of the Human Body.* Washington, DC: National Geographic Society, 2014.

WEBSITES

How the Body Works
kidshealth.org/kid/htbw/
Discover more about how the human body works here.

Organ Transplants
unos.org/docs/WEKNTK.pdf
Learn all about organ transplants from the United Network for Organ Sharing.

INDEX